I0842059

GRATEFULNESS

I am **GEORGE SARANGO** , Bachelor of Science Business man , and writer of books like **LEARNING ENGLISH** .
My gratefulness and dedication to my family for my 4 daughters Silvana, Evelin,
Lorent and Bea.

INDEX

LEARNING ENGLISH

INTRODUCTION

Welcome to "Learning English," a comprehensive guide designed to help you master the English language.

Whether you're a beginner just starting your journey or an intermediate learner looking to enhance your skills, this book is your trusted companion in the exciting world of English language acquisition.

English is the global language of communication, opening doors to countless opportunities in education, business, travel, and cultural exploration.

 Proficiency in English can significantly broaden your horizons, allowing you to connect with people from all corners of the world and access a wealth of knowledge and experiences.

In this book, we have carefully structured a step-by-step learning path that covers all aspects of the English language.

From fundamental grammar rules to advanced communication techniques, you'll find everything you need to become a confident and effective English speaker and writer.

What to Expect

Each chapter in this book is designed to provide you with a well-rounded understanding of English language skills.

We've included interactive exercises, practical examples, and engaging activities to make your learning experience enjoyable and effective.

Whether you're studying on your own or with a tutor, you'll find valuable resources and guidance to support your progress.

How to Use This Book

You can use this book in a way that suits your individual learning style and needs.

Feel free to start from the beginning and work your way through each chapter sequentially, or jump to specific sections that address your current goals and challenges.

The choice is yours.

Setting Your Goals

Before you dive into the content, take a moment to set your personal language learning goals.

Whether you aspire to master English for academic purposes, travel, business, or personal enrichment, having clear objectives will help you stay motivated and focused throughout your learning journey.

Remember that learning a new language is a gradual process, and patience is key.

 It's perfectly normal to encounter difficulties along the way, but with dedication and consistent effort, you will see remarkable progress.

Let's Begin!

Learning English is an adventure that opens doors to the world and enriches your life in countless ways.

We're excited to be your guide on this journey, and we're confident that with the right mindset and the resources provided in this book, you'll achieve your language learning goals.

So, without further ado, let's embark on this exciting path to mastering the English language.

Whether you're looking to improve your grammar, expand your vocabulary, or refine your conversational skills, this book is your trusted companion every step of the way.

Get ready to unlock the power of English and discover a world of opportunities that await you!

This book sets the tone for the book, emphasizing the importance of English language learning, the structure of the book, and the reader's role in setting and achieving their goals.

CHAPTER 1 INTRODUCTION TO LANGUAGE LEARNING

Section 1: The Power of Language Learning

The World of Languages: We begin by exploring the fascinating diversity of languages spoken around the world.

Readers are introduced to the idea that languages are not just tools for communication but also windows into different cultures and perspectives.

Why Learn English?: English, as one of the most

widely spoken languages globally, plays a crucial role in international communication, business, travel, and culture. In this section, we delve into the myriad of reasons why learning English is valuable and how it can open doors to opportunities.

Section 2: Your Language Learning Journey

Setting Language Learning Goals: We guide readers in understanding the importance of setting clear and achievable language learning goals.

Whether it's for personal growth, travel, academics, or career advancement, defining objectives is the first step towards successful language acquisition.

Assessing Your Current Proficiency: It's essential to have a baseline understanding of your current language skills.

We provide self-assessment tools and tips to help readers gauge their starting point.

Section 3: The Language Learning Process

Understanding Language Acquisition: This section explains the stages of language acquisition, from initial exposure to fluency.

We discuss the concept of language proficiency and the challenges learners might encounter along the way.

Effective Learning Strategies:

We introduce readers to various strategies for efficient language learning, including the importance of consistent practice, immersion, and using context to understand language.

Section 4: Tools and Resources

Choosing the Right Learning Materials: Selecting appropriate learning materials is crucial.

We provide guidance on how to choose textbooks, online courses, language apps, and other resources that align with individual learning styles and goals.

Creating a Supportive Learning Environment: Building an effective study space and time management are key to successful language learning.

Practical tips on organizing one's study environment are shared.

Section 5: Your Personal Language Learning Plan

Developing a Customized Learning Plan: We assist readers in creating a personalized language learning plan based on their goals, available resources, and preferred study methods.

A well-structured plan keeps learners motivated and focused.

Tracking Progress: Setting milestones, self-assessment, and journaling are introduced as tools to monitor and celebrate progress. Keeping track of one's development can boost motivation.

By the end of this introductory chapter, readers will have a solid understanding of the importance of learning English, clear goals to work towards, and a personalized plan to guide their language learning journey.

Learning a new language is an exciting and fulfilling endeavor, and with dedication, progress is achievable.

In the chapters that follow, we will delve deeper into the mechanics of the English language, starting with the basics of grammar in Chapter 2.

Together, we'll embark on an exciting adventure to master the English language and unlock a world of opportunities and connections.

This chapter provides readers with a strong foundation for their English language learning journey, including an understanding of the benefits of language proficiency, guidance on setting goals, insight into the language learning process, and practical tips for selecting resources and creating a personalized learning plan

CHAPTER 2 BASIC ENGLISH GRAMMAR

Section 1: Understanding the Structure of Sentences

Parts of Speech:

We begin by introducing the fundamental building blocks of sentences, including nouns, verbs, adjectives, adverbs, pronouns, prepositions, conjunctions, and interjections.

Readers will learn how each part of speech functions within a sentence.

Sentence Types:

We explore the four main types of sentences: declarative, interrogative, imperative, and exclamatory.

Examples and exercises help readers grasp the nuances of sentence structure.

Section 2: Nouns and Pronouns

Nouns: This section covers different types of nouns, such as common nouns, proper nouns, countable nouns, and uncountable nouns.

Readers will learn how to use nouns correctly in sentences.

Pronouns:

We discuss pronouns as substitutes for nouns, including personal pronouns, possessive pronouns, demonstrative pronouns, and reflexive pronouns.

Exercises reinforce proper pronoun usage.

Section 3: Verbs and Verb Tenses

Verbs:

We delve into the world of verbs, covering action verbs, linking verbs, auxiliary verbs, and verb phrases.

Readers will gain a solid understanding of how verbs function in sentences.

Verb Tenses:

This section introduces the concept of verb tenses, including present, past, and future tenses.

We provide clear explanations and practice exercises for each tense.

Section 4: Adjectives and Adverbs

Adjectives:

We explain how adjectives modify nouns and help provide more vivid descriptions.

Readers will learn about comparative and superlative forms of adjectives.

Adverbs:

This section explores adverbs, which modify verbs, adjectives, and other adverbs.

We cover the different types of adverbs and their placement in sentences.

Section 5: Sentence Structure and Word Order

Basic Sentence Structure:

Readers will understand the typical word order in English sentences, including subject-verb-object (SVO) and subject-object-verb (SOV) patterns.

Negation and Questions:

We cover how to form negative sentences and questions using auxiliary verbs.

Clear examples and exercises aid comprehension.

By the end of this chapter, readers will have a solid grasp of basic English grammar concepts.

They'll be able to identify and use different parts of speech, construct sentences with correct word order, and understand verb tenses and their usage.

A strong foundation in grammar is essential for effective communication in English.

In the following chapters, we will build upon this foundation and explore more advanced grammar topics and language skills.

Stay committed to your language learning journey, and remember that practice and consistency are key to mastering English grammar.

This chapter provides readers with a comprehensive understanding of basic English grammar, covering essential topics such as parts of speech, sentence structure, nouns, pronouns, verbs, adjectives, adverbs, and verb tenses.

Clear explanations and practical exercises help reinforce these fundamental concepts, setting the stage for more advanced language skills in subsequent chapters.

CHAPTER 3 BUILDING YOUR VOCABULARY

Section 1: The Importance of Vocabulary

The Vocabulary Advantage:

We start by highlighting the crucial role vocabulary plays in effective communication.

Readers will understand how a rich vocabulary enhances both spoken and written expression.

The Vocabulary-Learning Continuum:

We introduce the idea that vocabulary acquisition is an ongoing process that evolves over time.

Readers will discover that expanding their vocabulary is not a one-time effort but a continuous journey.

Section 2: Vocabulary Acquisition Strategies

Contextual Learning:

This section explores how words are learned in context.

We discuss strategies like reading extensively, watching movies, and listening to podcasts to encounter new words naturally.

Word Lists and Flashcards:

We introduce the concept of word lists and flashcards as valuable tools for vocabulary expansion.

Readers will learn how to create and use these aids effectively.

Section 3: Building Vocabulary Through Reading

Reading for Vocabulary Growth:

We delve into the benefits of reading as a primary means of vocabulary expansion.

Readers will discover how different types of reading materials can enhance their word knowledge.

Vocabulary in Literature:

This section highlights how classic and contemporary literature can expose readers to diverse vocabulary.

We provide examples from famous literary works to illustrate this point.

Section 4: Word Roots, Prefixes, and Suffixes

Understanding Word Origins:

We explore how many English words are derived from Latin, Greek, and other languages.

 Readers will learn how understanding word roots, prefixes, and suffixes can unlock the meanings of unfamiliar words.

Word Formation:

We discuss how adding prefixes and suffixes can change the meaning of words.

Practical exercises help readers practice word formation.

Section 5: Expanding Your Word Bank

Word-a-Day Challenge:

We introduce a fun and effective way to learn a new word every day. Readers will see how this simple habit can significantly boost their vocabulary.

Thematic Vocabulary Lists:

We provide thematic vocabulary lists related to various topics and contexts, such as travel, food, business, and technology.

These lists help readers target specific areas of interest.

Section 6: Using Vocabulary in Context

Conversational Vocabulary:

We discuss how to incorporate newly acquired vocabulary into everyday conversations.

Readers will learn practical tips for using words naturally and effectively.

Writing with Flair:

This section explores how to enrich writing with a broader vocabulary.

We provide examples of descriptive writing and show readers how to employ vivid language.

By the end of this chapter, readers will have a toolkit of strategies for expanding their vocabulary effectively.

They'll understand the benefits of contextual learning, word roots, and thematic lists.

With practice, they can build a diverse word bank that enhances their English language skills in both spoken and written communication.

In the following chapters,

we'll continue to reinforce vocabulary growth as we explore various language skills and applications.

Keep in mind that vocabulary development is a continuous journey, and the more words you acquire, the more confidently and eloquently you can express yourself in English.

This chapter provides readers with a comprehensive guide to building their English vocabulary.

It covers the importance of vocabulary, acquisition strategies, the role of reading, word roots and affixes, practical exercises, and tips for using newly acquired words in conversation and writing.

Building a strong vocabulary is essential for effective communication and language proficiency, and this chapter equips readers with the tools and techniques to do just that.

CHAPTER 4 SPEAKING AND PRONUNCIATION

Section 1: The Art of Effective Speaking

The Importance of Spoken Communication:

We begin by emphasizing the significance of effective spoken communication in various aspects of life, including social interactions, business, and academics.

Building Confidence:

Readers will learn strategies for building confidence in speaking, including overcoming anxiety, embracing mistakes, and setting realistic expectations.

Section 2: Developing Clear Pronunciation

Understanding Pronunciation:

We delve into the importance of clear pronunciation in communication.

Readers will gain an understanding of why pronunciation matters and how it impacts comprehension.

Phonetic Basics:

We introduce the International Phonetic Alphabet (IPA) and its role in understanding English sounds.

This section provides an overview of key English sounds and their symbols.

Section 3: Practicing Pronunciation

Common Pronunciation Challenges:

We identify common pronunciation challenges for English learners, such as consonant clusters, vowel sounds, and stress patterns.

Exercises for Clear Pronunciation:

This section offers a variety of exercises and drills to help readers

practice and improve their pronunciation.

Audio examples and repetition exercises are included.

Section 4: Conversation Skills and Fluency

Effective Communication:

We explore the elements of effective conversation, including active listening, turn-taking, and maintaining engagement in discussions.

Building Fluency:

Readers will learn techniques for improving fluency, including practicing with native speakers, participating in language exchanges, and using language learning apps for speaking practice.

Section 5: Understanding Accents and Dialects

Accents and Dialects:

We discuss the diversity of English accents and dialects around the world.

Readers will gain an appreciation for linguistic variations and how they can impact comprehension.

Accent Reduction Strategies:

This section provides tips and strategies for learners who wish to reduce their accent or adopt a neutral

English accent for clearer communication.

Section 6: Practical Speaking Exercises

Role-Playing Scenarios:

We offer role-playing scenarios for common real-life situations, such as ordering food at a restaurant, making phone calls, and participating in job interviews.

Group Discussions:

Readers will find guidance on how to facilitate and participate in group discussions, debates, and presentations in English.

By the end of this chapter, readers will have a solid foundation in the art of speaking and pronunciation in English

They will have improved their confidence, developed clear pronunciation skills, and practiced speaking in various contexts.

Effective spoken communication is a vital aspect of language learning, and this chapter equips readers with the knowledge and tools to become more confident and proficient speakers of English.

In the subsequent chapters, we will continue to refine language skills, explore reading comprehension, writing, listening, and more, all of which contribute to becoming a well-rounded English language learner.

This chapter provides readers with a comprehensive guide to speaking and pronunciation in English.

It covers the importance of effective spoken communication, strategies for building confidence, phonetic basics, pronunciation exercises, conversation skills, accent understanding, and practical speaking exercises.

Developing clear pronunciation and confident speaking skills is essential for effective communication in English, and this chapter equips readers with the knowledge and tools to do just that.

CHAPTER 5 READING COMPREHENSION

Section 1: The Importance of Reading

The Power of Reading:

We start by emphasizing the significant role that reading plays in language learning and overall cognitive development.

Readers will understand how reading expands vocabulary, enhances comprehension, and fosters critical thinking.

Types of Reading Materials:

This section introduces a variety of reading materials, including books, newspapers, magazines, websites, and more.

Readers will discover the different styles and genres available for practice.

Section 2: Strategies for Effective Reading

Active Reading Techniques:

We delve into active reading strategies, such as annotating, highlighting, and taking notes while reading.

Readers will learn how these techniques can improve comprehension and retention.

Vocabulary in Context:

This section discusses how to infer word meanings from context, an essential skill for expanding vocabulary.

Practical exercises guide readers in practicing this skill.

Section 3: Comprehension Skills

Understanding Main Ideas:

We introduce techniques for identifying the main idea and supporting details in a text.

Readers will learn how to extract essential information from passages.

Making Inferences:

This section explores how to make logical inferences based on information provided in the text.

Readers will practice drawing conclusions from reading materials.

Section 4: Reading Speed and Fluency

Improving Reading Speed:

We provide tips and exercises to help readers increase their reading speed while maintaining comprehension.

Speed reading techniques are introduced.

Building Reading Fluency:

Readers will learn how to enhance reading fluency, which involves reading smoothly and with expression.

Practice exercises aid in developing this skill.

Section 5: Analyzing Different Text Types

Fiction vs. Non-Fiction:

We discuss the differences between fiction and non-fiction texts and offer strategies for approaching each type effectively.

Reading Across Genres:

Readers will explore different genres, such as literature, history, science, and news articles, and learn how to adapt their reading strategies accordingly.

Section 6: Critical Reading and Beyond

Critical Reading:

This section introduces critical reading skills, such as evaluating arguments, identifying bias, and questioning assumptions.

Readers will develop a critical approach to reading.

Beyond Comprehension:

We discuss how reading comprehension extends beyond understanding the text to critical analysis, reflection, and application in real-life situations.

By the end of this chapter, readers will have honed their reading comprehension skills significantly.

They will be adept at active reading, extracting main ideas, making inferences, and reading different types of materials with ease.

Effective reading comprehension is a cornerstone of language learning, and this chapter equips readers with the strategies and techniques necessary to become proficient readers in English.

In the following chapters, we will continue to explore various language skills and applications, building upon the strong foundation established in this chapter.

This chapter provides readers with a comprehensive guide to reading comprehension in English.

It covers the importance of reading, strategies for effective reading, comprehension skills, reading speed, analysis of different text types, critical reading, and the application of reading skills.

Developing strong reading comprehension skills is essential for language acquisition and critical thinking, and this chapter equips readers with the knowledge and tools to excel in this area.

CHAPTER 6 WRITING SKILLS

Section 1: The Power of Effective Writing

The Significance of Writing:

We begin by highlighting the importance of writing skills in various aspects of life, including academics, business, and personal communication.

Readers will understand how well-developed writing skills enhance clarity and impact.

Types of Writing:

This section introduces different forms of writing, including essays, reports, emails, creative writing, and more.

Readers will explore the diverse purposes and styles associated with each type.

Section 2: The Writing Process

Planning and Organization: We discuss the importance of planning before writing.

Readers will learn how to outline ideas, set goals, and structure their writing effectively.

Drafting and Revising:

This section explores the process of writing drafts and the importance of revision. Readers will understand how to refine their writing for clarity and coherence.

Section 3: Grammar and Style

Grammar Basics:

**We provide a review of essential grammar rules, such as sentence structure, subject-verb agreement, and verb tense consistency. Practical exercises reinforce these concepts.

Writing Style:

This section covers writing style, including the use of active voice, clarity, conciseness, and tone. Readers will learn how to convey their intended message effectively.

Section 4: Building Strong Paragraphs and Essays

Constructing Effective Paragraphs:

We discuss the elements of a well-structured paragraph, including topic sentences, supporting details, and transitions. Readers will practice building cohesive paragraphs.

Essay Writing:

This section guides readers through the essay writing process, from selecting a topic and creating a thesis statement to developing arguments and providing evidence. Sample essays and essay planning exercises are included.

Section 5: Creative Writing

Exploring Creativity:

We introduce creative writing as a means of self-expression.

Readers will explore various forms of creative writing, including short stories, poetry, and personal essays.

Writing Prompts:

This section provides a collection of writing prompts to inspire creativity and encourage readers to explore their imagination through writing.

Section 6: Effective Business and Professional Writing

Email and Correspondence:

We discuss best practices for writing professional emails and business correspondence.

Readers will learn how to convey their message clearly and professionally.

Report and Proposal Writing:

This section covers report and proposal writing for business and academic purposes.

Readers will gain insight into structuring and formatting these documents.

By the end of this chapter, readers will have developed a strong foundation in writing skills.

They will understand the writing process, grammar and style, paragraph and essay construction, creative writing techniques, and effective business and professional writing.

Proficiency in writing is a valuable skill in English, and this chapter equips readers with the knowledge and tools to become confident and skilled writers.

In the following chapters, we will continue to refine language skills and explore additional aspects of English language learning.

This chapter provides readers with a comprehensive guide to writing skills in English.

It covers the importance of writing, the writing process, grammar and style, constructing paragraphs and essays, creative writing, and business and professional writing.

Developing strong writing skills is essential for effective communication and academic and professional success, and this chapter equips readers with the knowledge and techniques necessary to excel in this area.

CHAPTER 7   LISTENING AND COMPREHENSION

Section 1: The Vital Role of Listening

Listening as a Language Skill:

We begin by underscoring the crucial importance of listening in the language acquisition process.

Readers will understand how strong listening skills are the foundation for effective communication.

Real-Life Applications:

This section introduces various real-life situations where listening skills are paramount, such as understanding spoken instructions, participating in meetings, and enjoying media in English.

Section 2: Strategies for Effective Listening

Active Listening Techniques:

We delve into active listening strategies, including maintaining focus, taking notes, and asking clarifying questions.

Readers will learn how these techniques enhance comprehension.

Different Accents and Dialects:

We discuss the diversity of English accents and dialects worldwide and provide guidance on how to adapt to different speech patterns.

Section 3: Building Listening Comprehension

Listening to Different Media:

Readers will explore listening materials from diverse sources, including podcasts, radio broadcasts, news reports, and interviews.

We provide guidance on selecting appropriate listening materials.

Understanding Spoken Language:

This section covers strategies for understanding spoken language, such as recognizing context clues, identifying key points, and inferring meaning.

Section 4: Note-Taking and Summarizing

Effective Note-Taking:

We offer techniques for taking effective notes while listening, including abbreviations, symbols, and organization methods.

Sample notes and exercises are included.

Summarizing Information:

Readers will learn how to summarize spoken information concisely and accurately, a valuable skill for academic and professional settings.

Section 5: Listening Comprehension Challenges

Listening to Fast Speech:

We provide exercises and techniques to help readers improve their ability to understand fast-paced speech and conversations.

Dealing with Background Noise:

This section addresses the challenge of listening in noisy environments and offers strategies for filtering out distractions.

Section 6: Engaging with Authentic Materials

Authentic Listening Materials:

We encourage readers to engage with authentic English materials, such as movies, documentaries, and music, to further develop their listening skills.

Language Immersion:

Readers will discover how language immersion through media and cultural experiences can significantly enhance their listening comprehension.

By the end of this chapter, readers will have honed their listening and comprehension skills significantly.

They will be proficient in active listening techniques, adapting to different accents, understanding spoken language in various contexts, and summarizing information effectively.

Listening and comprehension are critical components of effective communication in English, and this chapter equips readers with the knowledge and tools to excel in this area.

In the subsequent chapters, we will continue to refine language skills and explore various aspects of English language learning.

This chapter provides readers with a comprehensive guide to listening and comprehension in English.

It covers the significance of listening, strategies for effective listening, building comprehension skills, note-taking, summarizing information, and engaging with authentic listening materials.

Proficiency in listening is essential for effective communication and understanding spoken language in various contexts, and this chapter equips readers with the knowledge and techniques necessary to excel in this area.

CHAPTER 8 ENGLISH FOR DAILY LIFE

Section 1: The Importance of Everyday English

The Role of Daily Communication:

We begin by emphasizing the significance of English for everyday life.

Readers will understand how English proficiency enhances their ability to navigate daily situations, both locally and while traveling.

Practical Scenarios:

This section introduces various real-life scenarios where English is commonly used, such as shopping, dining out, asking for directions, and socializing.

Readers will see how English can be a valuable tool in these situations.

Section 2: Vocabulary and Phrases for Everyday Situations

Essential Vocabulary:

We provide readers with a list of essential vocabulary words and phrases specific to daily life.

These words and expressions cover greetings, shopping, dining, transportation, and more.

Role-Playing Exercises:

Readers will engage in role-playing exercises to practice using everyday English in simulated scenarios.

These exercises encourage active learning and application of language skills.

Section 3: Making Appointments and Reservations

Scheduling Appointments:

This section guides readers on how to make appointments with doctors, dentists, and other professionals.

Sample dialogues and practical advice are included.

Booking Reservations:

We discuss the process of reserving tables at restaurants, booking hotel rooms, and securing tickets for events.

Readers will learn the vocabulary and etiquette associated with reservations.

Section 4: Grocery Shopping and Dining Out

Grocery Shopping:

We provide readers with vocabulary and phrases necessary for grocery shopping, including food items, quantities, and common questions at the store.

Dining Etiquette:

This section covers dining out, from ordering food and drinks to paying the bill.

Readers will understand restaurant etiquette and be prepared for various dining scenarios.

Section 5: Handling Emergencies and Health Concerns

Emergency Situations:

We discuss how to handle emergencies, including calling for help, providing basic information, and seeking medical assistance.

Healthcare Conversations:

Readers will learn how to describe symptoms, make medical appointments, and discuss health concerns with healthcare professionals.

Section 6: Cultural Awareness and Sensitivity

Cultural Differences:

We emphasize the importance of cultural sensitivity when using English in daily life.

Readers will learn how cultural norms and customs can impact communication.

Respectful Language:

This section provides guidance on using respectful and polite language when interacting with people from diverse backgrounds.

By the end of this chapter, readers will be well-prepared to use English effectively in their daily lives.

They will have acquired essential vocabulary and phrases, practiced real-life scenarios, and gained cultural awareness to navigate various situations confidently.

Proficiency in everyday English is a valuable skill for communication and cultural sensitivity.

In the following chapters, we will continue to explore more advanced language skills and applications, building upon the practical foundation established in this chapter.

This chapter equips readers with the language skills and cultural awareness necessary for navigating daily life using English.

It covers practical scenarios, essential vocabulary and phrases, role-playing exercises, and guidance on handling everyday situations such as making appointments, shopping, dining out, and dealing with emergencies.

Proficiency in everyday English is crucial for effective communication and cultural sensitivity in various contexts.

CHAPTER 9 ENGLISH FOR BUSINESS AND PROFESSIONAL COMMUNICATION

Section 1: The Importance of Business English

The Role of Business English:

We begin by highlighting the critical role that English plays in the global business environment.

Readers will understand how proficiency in business English can lead to career opportunities and international collaboration.

Communication in the Workplace:

This section introduces the significance of effective communication in the workplace, from emails and meetings to presentations and negotiations.

Section 2: Business Vocabulary and Terminology

Business Terminology:

We provide readers with a list of essential business vocabulary and terminology, including terms related to finance, marketing, management, and more.

Industry-Specific Vocabulary:

Readers will explore industry-specific vocabulary and phrases relevant to their career fields, such as healthcare, technology, finance, or hospitality.

Section 3: Written Communication in the Professional World

Email Etiquette:

This section covers the etiquette of professional email communication, including greetings, formalities, and formatting.

Readers will learn how to compose effective work-related emails.

Report Writing:

We discuss the essentials of report writing, from structuring a report to presenting data and findings professionally.

Sample reports and guidelines are included.

Section 4: Effective Business Meetings and Presentations

Meeting Preparation:

Readers will learn how to prepare for business meetings effectively, including setting agendas, sending invitations, and managing time efficiently.

Presentation Skills:

This section provides guidance on delivering effective presentations, including creating engaging slides, speaking confidently, and handling questions from the audience.

Section 5: Networking and Professional Relationships

Building Professional Networks:

We discuss the importance of networking in the business world and offer tips for building and maintaining professional relationships.

Negotiation and Conflict Resolution:

Readers will learn negotiation strategies and conflict resolution techniques, along with relevant vocabulary and phrases.

Section 6: Cross-Cultural Business Communication

Cultural Sensitivity:

We emphasize the significance of cultural awareness in international business communication.

Readers will learn how to navigate cultural differences respectfully and effectively.

Language for Global Business:

This section provides guidance on conducting business in an international context, including multilingual meetings and correspondence.

By the end of this chapter, readers will have acquired the language skills and knowledge necessary for effective business and professional communication in English.

They will be equipped with essential business vocabulary, email etiquette, report writing skills, meeting and presentation techniques, negotiation strategies, and cultural awareness.

In the final chapter, we will summarize the key takeaways from the book and encourage readers to continue their language learning journey with confidence.

This chapter equips readers with the language and communication skills required for success in the business and professional world.

It covers essential business vocabulary, email and report writing, meeting and presentation skills, networking, negotiation, and cultural sensitivity in business communication.

Proficiency in business English is a valuable asset for career growth and international collaboration.

CHAPTER 10 ADVANCED ENGLISH SKILLS

Section 1: The Journey to Advanced Proficiency

The Path to Mastery:

We begin by acknowledging the reader's progress and dedication to reaching an advanced level of English proficiency.

This section provides motivation for continued learning.

Setting Advanced Goals:

Readers will learn how to set specific advanced language learning goals tailored to their personal and professional aspirations.

Section 2: Advanced Vocabulary and Idioms

Expanding Your Lexicon:

We introduce advanced vocabulary words and idiomatic expressions that go beyond everyday language.

Readers will learn how to use these words and phrases effectively in both spoken and written English.

Contextual Usage:

This section emphasizes the importance of using advanced vocabulary and idioms appropriately in different contexts and registers.

Section 3: Complex Sentence Structures

Compound and Complex Sentences:

We delve into advanced sentence structures, including compound and complex sentences.

Readers will learn how to create more sophisticated sentences to express complex ideas.

Subordinate Clauses:

This section covers the use of subordinate clauses to add depth and nuance to writing and speaking.

Section 4: Advanced Reading and Analysis

Literary Analysis:

Readers will explore advanced reading comprehension techniques, including analyzing literature, identifying themes, and interpreting symbolism.

Critical Reading:

We discuss advanced critical reading skills, such as evaluating arguments, identifying bias, and recognizing rhetorical devices in texts.

Section 5: Advanced Writing Techniques

Persuasive Writing:

This section introduces persuasive writing techniques, including crafting arguments, using evidence effectively, and persuading readers through well-structured essays and reports.

Creative Writing Challenges:

Readers will engage in advanced creative writing challenges, such as crafting short stories, poetry, and essays that require complex themes and creative expression.

Section 6: Advanced Listening and Speaking

Listening to Authentic Materials:

We encourage readers to explore authentic English materials, such as podcasts, TED Talks, and academic lectures, to enhance their listening skills.

Advanced Speaking Practice:

Readers will engage in advanced speaking exercises, including debates, discussions on complex topics, and formal presentations.

Section 7: Preparing for Advanced Tests and Examinations

Test Strategies:

We provide strategies and tips for tackling advanced English proficiency tests, such as the TOEFL, IELTS, or advanced-level Cambridge exams.

Practice Exams:

This section includes sample questions and practice exams to help

readers assess their readiness for advanced English tests.

By the end of this chapter, readers will have reached an advanced level of English proficiency.

They will have expanded their vocabulary, mastered complex sentence structures, honed advanced reading and writing skills, improved listening and speaking abilities, and be prepared for advanced English tests and examinations.

The journey to advanced English proficiency is a remarkable achievement, and this chapter celebrates the reader's growth and encourages them to continue exploring and using the English language in diverse and meaningful ways.

This chapter serves as a culmination of the reader's English language learning journey, focusing on advanced language skills, including vocabulary, idioms, sentence structures, reading comprehension, writing techniques, listening, speaking, and test preparation.

It acknowledges the reader's progress and encourages them to continue using their advanced language skills in various contexts and for personal and professional development.

CONCLUSION

Concluding your Journey to English Mastery about this book LEARNING ENGLISH .

As we reach the end of this journey through "Learning English," it's essential to take a moment to reflect on the incredible progress you've made and the exciting possibilities that lie ahead.

Learning a new language is a remarkable achievement, and your dedication to mastering English is truly commendable.

Celebrating Your Achievements

Throughout this book, you've embarked on a comprehensive exploration of the English language, starting from the fundamentals of grammar and vocabulary, progressing through the development of crucial skills like speaking, reading, writing, and understanding spoken language.

You've navigated everyday scenarios and learned to communicate effectively in both personal and professional contexts.

From building a strong vocabulary to crafting persuasive essays, you've developed a versatile skill set that sets you on the path to language mastery.

The Continuation of Your Language Journey

Language learning is a lifelong adventure, and your journey with English doesn't end here.

As you move forward, consider these key points:

Consistent Practice:

Maintain a regular practice routine.

Continue reading, writing, speaking, and listening in English to reinforce and expand your skills.

Embrace Challenges:

Don't shy away from challenging content or complex language structures.

Push yourself to explore advanced materials and engage in meaningful conversations.

Stay Connected:

Engage with native speakers, join language communities, or seek out language exchange partners to stay connected with the language and culture.

Set New Goals:

As you achieve your current goals, set new ones.

Whether it's passing an advanced language proficiency exam, pursuing higher education in English, or excelling in your career, keep aiming higher.

Celebrate Progress:

Celebrate your language milestones, no matter how small.

Recognize your growth and the doors that English proficiency has opened for you.

The Global Opportunities of English

English is not just a language; it's a gateway to a world of opportunities.

Proficiency in English opens doors to international travel, cross-cultural experiences, academic pursuits, and global career prospects.

It allows you to connect with people from diverse backgrounds and share your ideas on a global stage. Your journey with English is a journey of empowerment and enrichment.

Thank You for Being a Part of This Journey

I want to extend my sincere gratitude for being a part of this learning experience.

Your dedication to improving your English skills is inspiring, and I hope this book has been a valuable companion on your language learning journey.

Remember, language learning is not just about mastering words and grammar; it's about connecting with people, understanding different cultures, and broadening your horizons.

As you continue your language adventure, embrace every moment of growth and enjoy the incredible journey that lies ahead.

Wishing you a future filled with endless opportunities, meaningful connections, and the joy of mastering the English language.

Keep exploring, keep learning, and keep shining on your path to English mastery.

Warmest regards,

[Your Name].................................

This conclusion wraps up the book with a message of celebration and encouragement for the reader's ongoing language learning journey.

It emphasizes the importance of consistent practice, setting new goals, and celebrating progress while highlighting the global opportunities that English proficiency offers.

It also expresses gratitude to the reader for their commitment to learning and encourages them to continue exploring the world through the English language.